STUDY WORKBOOK FOR ISBN 978-1933039640

Real Estate Title Search Abstractor Training

Library of Congress -in-Publication Data
October 2012

Real Estate Title Search Abstracting Study Workbook for ISBN 978-1933039640

Printed in the United States of America

10 9 8 7 6 5 4 3 2 1

Coursework is available at special quantity discounts to use as premiums and sales promotions within corporate or private training programs. To obtain information or inquire about availability please write to Director, PO Box 1, Hollidaysburg, PA 16648.

STUDY WORKBOOK FOR ISBN 978-1933039640

Real Estate Title Search Abstractor Training

Flashcard Set

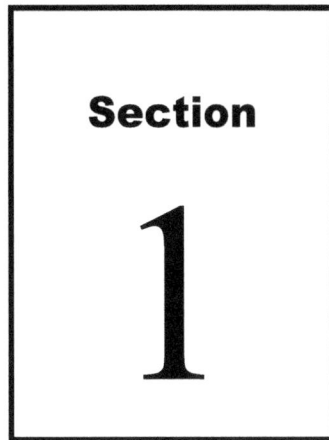

The flashcard set is designed to assist you in testing you retention of the materials. You should complete the coursework and then use a file card to cover the second row that contains the answers to each question.

Review the questions and then check your answers.

When you feel you are ready for enhanced testing, complete the self-test segments of the workbook. Completing the self-tests without reference to the written text is the best method of assessing your knowledge base. If you are unable to answer a particular question, you should review the applicable chapter in its entirety.

A competent title researcher must be able

- Document the status of any defects
- Review and establish a chain of title
- Carefully and accurately search public records
- All of the Above

A competent title abstractor must be able to document the status of any defects, review and establish a chain of title, carefully and accurately search public records.

The _____ is the written declaration of a statement of _____ that is made voluntarily and sworn to or affirmed before some person legally _____ to administer an oath or affirmation.

The affidavit is the written declaration of a statement of fact that is made voluntarily and sworn to or affirmed before some person legally authorized to administer an oath or affirmation.

Advanced abstracting duties might include

- the issuance of title policies
- the creation of title commitments
- the underwriting of specific issues to a property
- all of the above

Advanced Abstractor duties might include the issuance of title policies, the creation of title commitments, and the underwriting of specific issues to a property.

What is a Settlement?

The time at which a property transfer is finalized.

The severance of a resource right may be completed by

- Conveyance or grant
- A lease of the named rights
- Adverse possession
- All of the above

The severance of a resource right might be accomplished by conveyance or grant, a lease of the named rights, or adverse possession.

What is Title Insurance?

The insurance policy that agrees to indemnify the insured against defects in the title.

The title commitment will be dated with the _____ date and time that you noted as the _____ date and time for your abstracting summary.

The title commitment will be dated with the <u>same</u> date and time that you noted as the <u>completion</u> date and time for your abstracting summary.

What is Tenancy in Common?

A form of joint tenancy by two or more individuals or entities where each obtains an undivided interest in real property.

Sub-surface rights typically include the right to [all] of the following except

- The right to sell crop
- The right to enter beneath the surface of the land
- The right to lease mineral rights to another
- None of the above

Sub-surface rights do not include the right to sell crops. Crops are a part of the surface rights of a property.

What is the purpose of affirmative insurance?

The purpose of affirmative insurance is to insure over a specific defect lien, encumbrance or interest that affects the title.

Which item is typically not included with air rights?

• Electrical Wires
• Roofs
• Tree Limbs
• Air above the property

Air rights include the right to anything above a parcel of property, a roof is a part of the improvement and is included within surface rights.

What is a certificate of title?

A certificate of title is an opinion issued by an attorney detailing who rightfully owns a piece of land.

Possible transfers of airspace would include the sale of

- Navigational easements
- Mineral Rights
- Water rights
- Both A and C

A possible transfer of air rights might be the granting of a navigational easement.

Surface rights are commonly referred to as:

- The right to the land and the improvements of the land
- The right to what is beneath the land
- The right to what is above the land
- All of the above

Surface rights are commonly referred to as the right to the land and the improvements of the land.

Improvements may include

- Pipelines
- Pavement
- Buildings
- All of the above

Improvements may include pipelines, pavement, and buildings on the land.

What is the Bundle of Rights?

All rights of ownership of real property. Synonym for estate.

Which of the following is not considered real property?

- A dresser
- Trees
- A fence
- None of the above

A dresser is an item of personal property and will not be included within the transfer of real property.

What is an acknowledgement?

A declaration made before a notary or other official certifying that the signing of a document is of a voluntary act undertaken of ones own free will.

What standard is not applied when determining if an item is a fixture?

- The interpretation of a real estate agent
- The intention of the parties who own the property
- The manner in which the item is attached to the real property
- An agreement between the parties in the transaction

The interpretation of a real estate agent is not a valid method of determining if an item is a fixture.

What is not typically a reason an owner might sever a specific right from the bundle of rights?

- To build additional structures
- To reduce taxes
- To create a leaseback transaction
- To increase the value of a property

An owner might sever the bundle of rights to reduce taxes, create a leaseback transaction, or increase the value of a property. An owner does not need to sever the bundle of rights to build an additional structure on the property.

What is an abstract of title?

The chronological history of the most relevant parts of every recorded instrument regarding a title.

An informal reference is

• Numbers and names of streets used to describe a property
• A monument set at one corner of a parcel
• Degrees, minutes and seconds
• All of the above

An informal reference are the numbers and names of streets used to describe a property.

A rectangular survey uses

• Degrees
• Principal Meridians
• Lot-Block Tracts
• All of the Above

A rectangular survey uses Principal Meridians.

What is a Cloud on the Title?

A claim, document, defect, or discrepancy that casts doubt on the marketability of a title.

Which of the following includes the current owner's name, address and the assessed value of the improvements to the property?

- Recorded Plat
- Assessor's Parcel
- Metes and Bounds
- All of the above

The Assessor's Parcel includes the current owner's name, address and the assessed value of the improvements to the property.

A survey drawing does not show

- Improvements
- Easements
- Features
- Mortgages

A survey does not show mortgages relating to the property.

What survey method uses degrees, minutes and seconds?

- Rectangular survey
- Recorded plat
- Metes and Bounds
- None of the Above

The Metes and Bounds method uses degrees, minutes and seconds.

An acre contains how many square feet?

- 49,650
- 33,650
- 43,650
- 39,650

A acre contains 43,650 square feet.

A square mile contains how many square acres?

- 640
- 650
- 540
- None of the Above

A square mile contains 640 square acres.

What term describes the situation where a property touches another piece of real estate or a public road?

- Legal access
- Physical access
- Abut
- All of the Above

When a property touches another piece of real estate or a public road it is said to abut that area. Your search should verify the legal access of the property to the adjacent item.

An additional right that may be granted to
a property bordering water is

- Riparian right
- Accretion Right
- Egress
- All of the Above

A property bordering water may have a
riparian right.

What is an endorsement?

An addition that either expands or limits
the standard coverage provided under
a title insurance policy.

The alteration to a waterway for individual use may be allowed under the doctrine of prior appropriation.

- True
- False

TRUE - The alteration to a waterway for individual use may be allowed under the doctrine of prior appropriation

If a right of way is not visible in any public record, you should consult with the underwriter assigned to the file to determine what additional items of research may be required.

- True
- False

TRUE - If a right of way is not visible in any public record, you should consult with the underwriter assigned to the file to determine what additional items of research may be required.

What is Quiet Title?

A Quiet Title suit is a court action to obtain a determination regarding ownership right.

If a property abuts a road, it automatically gains access to that road.

- True
- False

FALSE – Just because a property touches a road does not mean it is automatically granted legal access. You must prove that the right to legally access a road is granted within the public records.

A matter that impairs the right of access to a property must be

- covered under easement insurance
- noted and specifically excepted in schedule B
- linked to an adjoining property
- all of the above

A matter that impairs the right of access to a property must be noted and specifically excepted in schedule B of the title insurance policy.

Rights may be fully bundled at the time of transfer

- True
- False

TRUE – Rights may be fully bundled at the time of the transfer of real property or an action may have been taken to sever one or more rights.

Ownership in the freehold estate ends at the owner's death.

- True
- False

FALSE – Ownership in a freehold estate does NOT end with the owner's death. Ownership in a freehold estate is inheritable.

What type of estate is contingent on the occurrence of a specific event?

- Life Estate
- Determinable Fee Estate
- Leasehold Estate
- All of the above

A Life Estate, Determinable Fee Estate, and Leasehold Estate are all estate types that are contingent on the occurrence of a specific event.

What is a Certificate of Title?

A certificate of title is evidence of the title status.

The government retains what right in the US ownership and transfer?

- Taxation
- Police Power
- Escheat
- All of the above

The government retains the right to Taxation, Police Power, and Escheat. The remaining rights are given to the individual owner.

What is an easement?

The right of a person to use the land of another.

Title is a synonym for

• Bundle of rights
• Ownership
• Eminent Domain
• None of the Above

Title is synonymous with ownership.

Fee simple estates are not inheritable.

- True
- False

FALSE – Fee Simple estates are inheritable.

The chain of title is complete when all events are _____ from the original source of title to the present owner. If there is a _____ _____, the current owner does not have _____ title to the property.

The chain of title is complete when all events are <u>documented</u> from the original source of title to the present owner. If there is a <u>missing link</u>, the current owner does not have <u>valid</u> title to the property.

When you locate an encumbrance, you should make a mental note in the event it becomes an issue at a later date

- True
- False

FALSE - When you locate an encumbrance, you should describe the details of the document within the abstracting report.

If unpaid inheritance taxes exist, you should

- Note the existence on your report
- Request an exception on the title commitment
- Request the taxes be paid according to statute
- Any of the Above

If unpaid inheritance taxes exist, you should note the existence and details within the abstracting report.

When researching estates, you should focus on

- the acts of the current owner
- the acts of the previous owners
- the tax payment status
- all of the above

All of the Above – When researching title, you should focus on ANY matter than may affect the rights inherent to the property.

A bundle of rights is

- the level of interest one loses to police power
- the level of interest one has in real property
- the interest a property owner has after a sale
- none of the above

The bundle of rights is the level of interest one has in real property.

The bundle of rights cannot be broken.

- True
- False

FALSE – The bundle of rights can be broken and it is an essential element of the search process to determine the status of the bundle of rights.

Limitations in the owner's rights may be imposed by

- Public Sources
- Private Sources
- Both public and private sources
- None of the above

Limitations in the owner's rights may be imposed by both public and private sources.

What is an amendment?

A change made to correct an error or to alter an agreement.

Government condemnation can be created by

• a deed restriction
• an easement
• a flood zone
• all of the above

Government condemnation can be created by a deed restriction, an easement, or an act of police power.

It is the job of the abstractor to determine what limitations are imposed on the bundle of rights.

- True
- False

TRUE – you must locate and document any limitations that are imposed on the bundle of rights.

What is a Specific Lien?

A specific lien against a particular piece of property.

Real estate taxes provide funds for

- upcoming elections
- special interest projects
- public benefits
- all of the above

Real estate taxes provide funds for services that benefit the public.

- The abstractor should note the

- location and description of an easement
- the wording of an easement
- the parties granting and gaining an easement
- all of the above

The abstractor should note the location and description of an easement, the exact wording of an easement, and the parties granting and gaining an easement.

What is a Preliminary Title Report?

A preliminary title is a report indicating the present condition of the title based on items discovered during a record search.

It is important that the abstractor fully note and describe any limitations discovered while researching the chain of title.

- True
- False

TRUE - It is important that the abstractor fully note and describe any limitations discovered while researching the chain of title.

An abstractor does not need to locate the final status of limitations including easements if they have adequately documented the wording and location of the information.

• True
• False

FALSE – An abstractor must always locate and document the status of any limitations, including easements.

Tenancy by Severalty means there

• Are 2 owners
• Are multiple Owners
• Is 1 Owner
• Any of the Above

Tenancy by Severalty means the property is owned by one owner.

Concurrent owners share

- The property
- Unity
- Ownership interest
- All of the Above

Concurrent owners share the property, unity and ownership interest in the property.

Any owner of a property may

- Incur liens
- Convey interest
- Create a condemnation
- All of the Above

Any owner of a property may incur liens, convey interest, or create a condemnation.

What type of lien is created against a property when an owner uses it as collateral to borrower money?

- General Lien
- Voluntary Lien
- Involuntary Lien
- All of the Above

A voluntary lien is created against a property when an owner uses it as collateral to borrower money.

A general lien goes against an individual and does not impact real property.

- True
- False

A general lien may affect any real estate owned by the individual who is the subject of the lien.

Which of the following best describes a real estate property tax lien?

- Voluntary Lien
- General Lien
- Specific Lien
- Any of the Above

A real estate tax lien is a specific lien against the property assessed.

When a property is sold by order of the court it is termed a

- Judgment Lien
- Foreclosure
- Escheat
- All of the Above

When a property is sold by order of the court is it termed a foreclosure.

Liens may be imposed against

• Fixtures
• Improvements
• Real Property
• All of the Above

Liens may be imposed against fixtures, improvements and real property.

Tax liens are similar to mechanics liens and voluntary liens in that they are recorded and paid in order of priority.

• True
• False

Tax liens are not subject the order of priority and take precedence over other liens regardless of the order of the recording.

A general warranty deed is the lowest form of deed.

- True
- False

FALSE – A general warranty deed is the highest form of deed.

A quitclaim deed

- contains no warranties
- contains no covenants
- does not promise the seller even holds interest in the property
- all of the above

A quitclaim deed contains no warranties, covenants, or even the promise that the individual signing the deed holds any interest in the property.

A cession deed is a form of

- General Warranty Deed
- Quitclaim Deed
- Guardians Deed
- None of the Above

A cession deed is a form of Quitclaim Deed.

A deed restriction may limit

- the action of a lender
- the action of the owner
- the action of an investor
- all of the above

A deed restriction may limit the actions of any party gaining ownership or other interest in a property.

The abstractor should review all documents and note any exception, restriction or other matter that may limit the rights of an owner.

- True
- False

TRUE - The abstractor should review all documents and note any exception, restriction or other matter that may limit the rights of an owner.

Unless an issue arises, deeds are the only legal documents you must review in the title search process.

- True
- False

FALSE – You must review all items in the public records that relate to the property you are researching.

You can confirm that a sales contract was terminated by locating

- proof of the sale and acquisition by the buyer named
- a judicial decree terminating the contract
- a recording instrument terminating the contract
- any of the above

You can confirm that a sales contract was terminated by locating proof of the sale and acquisition by the buyer named, a judicial decree terminating the contract, or a a recorded instrument terminating the contract.

What protection does title insurance offer?

Title insurance protects against losses that may arise from title defects that are not the fault of the abstractor and from title defects that were not located by the abstractor during the examination.

When a contract for deed exists,
    you should note

- the existence of the contract
- the parties to the contract
- the condition of the contract
- all of the above

When a contract for deed exists, you
should note the existence of the
contract, the parties to the contract,
and the condition of the contract

What does it mean to execute?

To validate a document.

If a contract that has not been terminated exists in record, options may include

- obtaining a judicial decree
- obtaining a seller declaration of forfeiture
- obtaining an executed release from the buyer
- any of the above

If a contract that has not been terminated exists in record, options may include obtaining a judicial decree, obtaining a seller declaration of forfeiture, or obtaining an executed release from the buyer.

An option may be removed from exception requirements if

- option has expired
- the underwriter deems the risk at a low level
- the option holder has died
- any of the above

An option may be removed from exception requirements if the option has expire, the underwriter deems the risk at a low level, or the option holder has died.

What is a Judgment?

The order by a court as to money owed or other definitive decisions.

A Grantor Index are formatted

• As one page per grantor
• Alphabetically
• Chronologically
• All of the Above

A Grantor Index are formatted as one page per grantor and arranged chronologically and alphabetically.

A chain of title is a record that links all previous lenders in order of priority.

- True
- False

FALSE – The chain of title is all recorded actions relating to a particular piece of property.

What is Marketable Title?

A title that is clear of liens, encumbrances and other defects.

Your search function will be contained only to those documents located within the recorder's office.

- True
- False

FALSE – Your search function will be contained to those items within the Public Records. These records may be stored in various locations, and not limited to the Record's office.

A break in the chain of title may occur as a result of

- a judicial determination not filed for record
- insufficient deeds of conveyance
- missing deeds or other documents
- all of the above

A break in the chain of title may result from a number of causes including a judicial determination not filed for record, insufficient deeds of conveyance, or missing deeds or other documents.

A break in the chain of title must be

- specifically excepted in the records
- remedied through the proper procedures
- noted and the next link in the chain researched
- any of the above

A break in the chain of title must be noted and the next link in the chain researched and then specifically excepted in the records or remedied through the proper procedures.

A defect in the title might be a result of the improperly recorded termination of a

- marriage
- judgment
- lien
- any of the above

The improper termination of a marriage, judgment, or lien may cause a break in the chain of title.

Prior to considering an abstract
complete, you must research

- Local Tax Rolls
- Lis Pendens Indexes
- Mechanic's Liens
- All of the above

Prior to considering an abstract
complete, you must research all public
records including Local Tax Rolls, Lis
Pendens Indexes, and Mechanic's
Liens.

If a defect exists, your responsibility is
to note the applicable data within
your report so the underwriter may
determine the handling of the defect.

- True
- False

TRUE - If a defect exists, your
responsibility is to note the applicable
data within your report so the
underwriter may determine the
handling of the defect.

If a defect exists, you should

- determine if the defect still exists and make the proper notation
- detail any alterations that occurred with regard to the defect
- note the method, time and processes that eliminated the defect
- all of the above

If a defect exists you should make the proper notation, detail any alterations that occurred with regard to the defect, and note the method, time and processes that eliminated the defect if these exist.

An abstract of title will include

- a historical summary of the chain of title
- the status of any defects that exist in the chain of title
- a comprehensive explanation of any item of issue in the chain of title
- all of the above

An abstract of title will include a historical summary of the chain of title, the status of any defects that exist in the chain of title, and a comprehensive explanation of any item of issue in the chain of title.

The abstractor will

- summarize each document located within the record
- note the book and page of each document located within the record
- note the date of each document entered into record
- all of the above

The abstractor will summarize each document located within the record, and note the date of the entry, the book, and the page of each document located within the record.

What is a Commitment of Title?

The guarantee from a title company that they will provide title insurance.

Title insurance is designed to protect

- against issues that come to light after the completion of the abstract
- the abstractor
- the insurance holder
- all of the above

Title insurance is designed to protect the insured, the title abstractor, and other interested party against issues that may have been missed during the search process or that come to light after the search is complete.

The title insurance process begins with

- the title underwriter examining the file to determine suitability to the companies guidelines
- the title attorney issuing an opinion as to the owner's rights to be transferred
- the title abstractor examining public records to determine the status of the title
- none of the above

The title insurance process begins with the title abstractor examining public records to determine the status of the title.

The title exam includes

- a review of the chain of title
- specifics of any defects encountered during research
- information regarding the status of any defects encountered
- all of the above

The title exam includes a review of the chain of title, specifics of any defects encountered during research, and information regarding the status of any defects encountered.

How does title insurance differ from traditional insurance?

Title insurance protects against events that have happened in the past while traditional insurance protects against possible future events.

The date and time you completed the abstract must be noted because

- additional issues may arise following your abstract report
- you must confirm the length of the search term
- the insurance premiums will be based upon the time of your search
- none of the above

The date and time you complete the abstracting report should be noted because additional matters may become part of public records following the completion of your search that create a blemish.

Title insurance issuance will be based on

- the status of the purchaser
- the completion of a search and exam of public records
- the lender's assessment of borrower suitability
- all of the above

Title insurance issuance will be based on the completion of a search and exam of public records.

Title insurance insures against future occurrences rather than past events

- True
- False

FALSE – Title insurance protects against PAST events.

What is an encumbrance?

Any item that affects the title to real property such as liens, easements, or deed restrictions.

When you discover a defect in the title insurance cannot be issued

- True
- False

FALSE – A defect may need to be corrected, excepted, or insured over but it is possible for a property owner to obtain a title insurance policy even if a defect exists within the title. The underwriter will make a determination as to whether insurance can be issued and what exceptions will be incorporated into the policy.

The chain is arranged _____ from the initial government patent or original source of the title to the present _____.

The chain is arranged <u>consecutively</u> from the initial government patent or original source of the title to the present <u>titleholder</u>.

Provide two reasons that an abstract might contain faulty data without the responsibility being the abstractors.

A married person represents himself on the deed, as a single person the deed may be invalidated.

A minor might have executed the deed causing potential validity questions.

An incompetent person may have executed the deed causing the validity of the deed to be called into question.

The deed may contain erroneous descriptions.

What basic items does the title exam report?

Chain of Title
Breaks in the Chain of Title
Defects in Title
Status of Defects

Schedule B of the title commitment will contain

- The policies and commitment coverage's
- The matters that affect the land as detailed in the legal description
- General, standard, and special exceptions to coverage
- All of the Above

Schedule B of the title commitment will contain General, standard, and special exceptions to coverage

---

What is the title search?

A check of title records to ensure that the seller is the legal owner of a property and that there are no liens or other claims against the property.

At times, mistakes in the preparation of the abstract may not be the fault of the abstractor conducting the search.

- True
- False

TRUE – At times mistakes in the abstract of title report may not be the fault of the title abstractor.

A chain of title is a compilation of what?

A chain of title is a compilation of all real estate instruments and other matters of record that effect the title of a particular piece of land.

Section

2

Skill Enhancement Self-Tests

Name:
Real Estate Title Search Abstractor
Abstracting Overview - Review Questions
Score:
Instructor:

1.   A title search must have the ability to:

2.   Advanced abstracting duties might include:

3.   Give the three characteristics most frequently sought in a title abstractor:

4.   Give the three most common career choices for a newly trained title abstractor:

5.   The primary concern of a title abstractor is:

_____
_____
_____
_____
_____

6.   Your abstract of title will include activities that affect the title from:

_____
_____
_____
_____
_____

7.   The primary duty of a title abstractor is:

_____
_____
_____
_____
_____

8.   What two specific determinations will be made based upon your abstracting report?

_____
_____
_____
_____
_____

9.   _____ and _____ base their entire
        process around the work that you perform during your research

10.   The career of real estate title abstractor is _____ to the _____ of the
        real estate title insurance and closing industries and as such requires _____,
        _____, and _____ practices on your part.

11.   A competent title researcher must be able to

        a.   document the status of any defects
        b.   review and establish a chain of title
        c.   carefully and accurately search public records
        d.   all of the above

12. Advanced abstracting duties might include

    a.   the issuance of title policies
    b.   the creation of title commitments
    c.   the underwriting of specific issues to a property
    d.   all of the above

13. An abstractor does not need to

    a.   provide dedication to the concise completion of each task
    b.   provide a methodical approach to task completion
    c.   customize their business process around their lifestyle
    d.   bring high levels of focus to their workflow

14. Positions in the title industry are

    a.   rewarding
    b.   secure
    c.   flexible
    d.   all of the above

15. Gaining an understanding of the overall task is more important than an attention to detail.

    a.   True
    b.   False

Name:
Real Estate Title Search Abstractor
Chapter 1 – Real Property Review Questions
Score:
Instructor:

1.   What are the three rights that may be transferred or severed from the transfer of land?

2.   Name the four standards to be applied when determining if an item is considered a fixture:

3.   Explain a reason that a fixture might not be insurable as part of the title commitment even when the real property contains no liens:

4.   The term severance when applied to real property rights and interests means:

5. Real property _____ rights include the _____ that exist and area actually _____ to the surface of the land.

6. A _____ is a piece of personal property that has been _____, _____ OR _____ _____ to a parcel of land or the structures on the land.

7. Crops are also known as _____ or _____.

8. A property's _____ is effected its ability to transfer _____ _____ to the new purchaser.

9. Sub-surface resources are subject to the same rights of _____ as any _____ portion of the land.

10. If an item is classified as _____ _____, it will not be included in the sale of real property.

11. The severance of a resource right may be completed by

    a.   Conveyance or grant
    b.   A lease of the named rights
    c.   Adverse possession
    d.   All of the above

12. Sub-surface rights typically include the right to all of the following except:

    a.   The right to sell crops
    b.   The right to enter beneath the surface of the land
    c.   The right to lease mineral rights to another
    d.   All of the above

13. Which item is typically not included with air rights?

    a. Electrical Wires
    b. Roofs
    c. Tree Limbs
    d. Air above the property

14. Possible transfers of airspace would include the sale of

    a. Navigational easements
    b. Mineral Rights
    c. Water rights
    d. Both A and C

15. Which of the following does not describe land rights?

    a. It is possible for one person to own the air rights and subsurface rights only
    b. A person can own the surface rights exclusively
    c. Only a company or the government can own mineral rights
    d. A person can own air, surface and sub-surface rights independently

16. Surface rights are commonly referred to as:

    a. The right to the land and the improvements of the land
    b. The right to what is beneath the land
    c. The right to what is above the land
    d. All of the above

17. Improvements may include:

    a. Pipelines
    b. Pavement
    c. Buildings
    d. All of the above

18. Which of the following is not considered real property?

    a. A dresser
    b. Trees
    c. A fence
    d. None of the above

19.   What standard is not applied when determining if an item is a fixture?

    a.   The interpretation of a real estate agent
    b.   The intention of the parties who own the property
    c.   The manner in which the item is attached to the real property
    d.   An agreement between the parties in the transaction

20.   What is not typically a reason an owner might sever a specific right from the bundle of rights?

    a.   To build additional structures
    b.   To reduce taxes
    c.   To create a leaseback transaction
    d.   To increase the value of a property

1.   Name the methods of land descriptions you will encounter during the title search
      process.

2.   The method that provides land description through street numbers and place names is
      known as INFORMAL REFERENCE and the primary advantage of this method of
      description is:

3.   Direction is shown as:

4.   The point where a parcel survey begins is frequently termed the:

5.   The RECTANGULAR SUVEY SYSTEM is also termed:

6.   What method of surveying is used to describe the most landmass in the United States?

7.   A check or quadrangle contains how many miles?

8.   Define a survey:

9.   Who sets the standards and requirements for surveyors in the United States?

10.   The _____ method begins at a _____, which is a permanent reference mark.

11.   Distance and direction is another term for _____ ___ _____ _____.

12.   It is customary to describe a parcel by going _____.

13.   Latitude lines run _____-_____ while longitude lines run _____-_____.

14.   Another term for the lot-block-tract system is the _____. _____.

15.   The _____ _____ _____ is a number assigned by the tax assessor to aid in tax collection.

16.   An informal reference is

        a.   Numbers and names of streets used to describe a property
        b.   A monument set at one corner of a parcel
        c.   Degrees, minutes and seconds
        d.   All of the above

17.   How many people will typically conduct a survey?

        a.   1
        b.   3
        c.   2
        d.   All of the above

18. A rectangular survey uses

    a. Degrees
    b. Principal Meridians
    c. Lot-Block Tracts
    d. All of the above

19. Which survey method uses a unit of measurement termed checks?

    a. Rectangular survey
    b. Metes and Bounds survey
    c. Recorded Plat survey
    d. All of the above

20. What method is most frequently used to define a parcel?

    a. Rectangular Survey
    b. Metes and Bounds
    c. Recorded Plat
    d. None of the above

21. Which of the following includes the current owner's name, address and the assessed value of the improvements to the property?

    a. Recorded Plat
    b. Assessor's Parcel
    c. Metes and Bounds
    d. All of the above

22. A survey drawing does not show

    a. Improvements
    b. Easements
    c. Features
    d. Mortgages

23. What survey method uses degrees, minutes and seconds?

    a. Rectangular survey
    b. Recorded plat
    c. Metes and Bounds
    d. None of the above

24. An acre contains how many square feet?

    a. 49,650
    b. 33,650
    c. 43,650
    d. 39,650

25. A square mile contains how many square acres?

    a. 640
    b. 650
    c. 540
    d. All of the above

Name:
Real Estate Title Search Abstractor
Chapter 2 – Access and Rights Review Questions
Score:
Instructor:

1.   All access points relating to the property being researched should:

2.   Physical access is:

3.   Legal access is:

4.   When you begin your research activity with regard to access it is best to:

5.   Define accretion

6.   List the three items you must specifically research in relationship to beach property.

7.   A riparian right is a right that occurs when a property borders a _____ or
        _____.

8.   A littoral right is a right that occurs when a property borders a _____ OR
        _____.

9.   The _____ of _____ _____ may
        come into effect that allows the first landowner that diverts water for his use to continue
        this diversion although it is not fair to other landowners.

10.   A common _____ would be an _____ or right-of-
        way that was gained for that particular parcel of land.

11.   What term describes the situation where a property touches another piece of real estate
        or a public road?

        a.   Legal access
        b.   Physical access
        c.   Abut
        d.   All of the above

12. The most common situations that create boundary line issues include

    a.   Improper location of fences
    b.   Accreted land
    c.   Defective legal descriptions
    d.   All of the above

13. An additional right that may be granted to a property bordering water is

    a.   Riparian right
    b.   Accretion Right
    c.   Egress
    d.   All of the above

14. The alteration to a waterway for individual use may be allowed under the doctrine of prior appropriation

    a.   True
    b.   False

15. The most common boundary line problems occur due to

    a.   Errors in surveys
    b.   Riparian rights
    c.   Abutters rights
    d.   All of the above

16. If a right of way is not visible in any public record, you should consult with the underwriter assigned to the file to determine what additional items of research may be required.

    a.   True
    b.   False

17. If a property abuts a road, it automatically gains access to that road.

    a.   True
    b.   False

18. A matter that impairs the right of access to a property must be

    a.   covered under easement insurance
    b.   noted and specifically excepted in schedule B
    c.   linked to an adjoining property
    d.   all of the above

19. An abstractor's only concern with regard to access to a property is whether it is accessible by vehicle.

    a.   True
    b.   False

20. If an issue exists with regard to tax assessment or property description, you must note the proper exception on the errors in survey report.

    a.   True
    b.   False

1.   Name the two parties who obtain rights to property:

2.   Define the term encumbrance.

3.   Explain the use of inheritance tax.

4.   Explain the use of estate tax.

5. The system of governing estates in the US most closely resembles the
_____ _____.

6. The highest and most complete form of estate ownership is the _____
_____, which is typically transferred using a _____
_____ _____.

7. A life estate provides a _____ _____ to use and occupy a
property and when it ends, the estate reverts to the original grantor who is also known as
the _____.

8. The concept of real estate ownership can be easiest understood when you view
ownership as a _____ ____ _____ or collection of rights to
ownership.

9. The abstract report is specifically concerned with rights that are _____ as well
as rights that are _____ in a real estate transfer.

10. If a person dies without a will or having disposed of their property, the laws of intestacy
property will come into effect. This is also known as the _____ _____
_____ _____ _____.

11. Rights may be fully bundled at the time of transfer

   a.   True
   b.   False

12. Our system of land management most closely resembles

   a.   feudal system
   b.   fee tail estate
   c.   Allodial system
   d.   reversionary estate

13. Ownership in the freehold estate ends at the owner's death

    a.   True
    b.   False

14. What type of estate is contingent on the occurrence of a specific event?

    a.   Life Estate
    b.   Determinable Fee Estate
    c.   Leasehold Estate
    d.   All of the above

15. The government retains what right in the US ownership and transfer?

    a.   Taxation
    b.   Police Power
    c.   Escheat
    d.   All of the above

16. Title is a synonym for

    a.   Bundle of rights
    b.   Ownership
    c.   Eminent Domain
    d.   None of the above

17. Fee simple estates are not inheritable

    a.   True
    b.   False

18. When another obtains a claim against a persons estate is a (n)

    a.   Escheat
    b.   Encumbrance
    c.   Domain
    d.   None of the above

19. When you locate an encumbrance, you should make a mental note in the event it becomes an issue at a later date

   a. True
   b. False

20. If unpaid inheritance taxes exist, you should

   a. Note the existence on your report
   b. Request an exception on the title commitment
   c. Request the taxes be paid according to statute
   d. Any of the above

21. When researching estates, you should focus on

   a. the acts of the current owner
   b. the acts of the previous owners
   c. the tax payment status
   d. all of the above

22. If a person dies without a valid will, you should

   a. Make a note for the underwriter
   b. Confirm the statutes of descent and distribution were followed
   c. Review the invalid will and note any issues for the underwriter
   d. All of the above

1.   The term bundle of rights refers to:

2.   Name four rights retained by the government.

3.   Explain how a deed restriction or _____ may be enforced.

4.   Give the explanation for an easement by prescription:

5. The government right of _____ _____ is imposed to protect the health, _____ and _____ _____ of the public.

6. An example of government _____ ___ _____ occurs when the government is acting to control a flood area and runs a drainage pipe _____ or _____ another's property.

7. The non-payment of _____ _____ may result in the government seizure of property resulting in the loss of an owner's interest. This occurs in an attempt to gain the needed revenue for specific operations.

8. The process of _____ _____ is the taking of a piece of private property for _____ _____.

9. If an individual loses the ability to enjoy full use of his property through the actions of another, he may bring an _____ _____ suit.

10. An easement grants the right to _____ _____ a certain portion of privately owned property.

11. A bundle of rights is

    a. the level of interest one loses to police power
    b. the level of interest one has in real property
    c. the interest a property owner has after a sale
    d. none of the above

12. The bundle of rights cannot be broken.

    a. True
    b. False

13. It is the job of the abstractor to determine what limitations are imposed on the bundle of rights

    a. True
    b. False

14. Limitations in the owner's rights may be imposed by

    a. Public Sources
    b. Private Sources
    c. Both public and private sources
    d. None of the above

15. Government condemnation can be created by

    a. a deed restriction
    b. an easement
    c. a flood zone
    d. all of the above

16. Real estate taxes provide funds for

    a. upcoming elections
    b. special interest projects
    c. public benefits
    d. all of the above

17. An integral part of the abstractor function is verification of the status of the taxes

    a. True
    b. False

18. The abstractor should note the

    a. location and description of an easement
    b. the wording of an easement
    c. the parties granting and gaining an easement
    d. all of the above

19. It is important that the abstractor fully note and describe any limitations discovered while researching the chain of title.

    a.   True
    b.   False

20. An abstractor does not need to locate the final status of limitations including easements if they have adequately documented the wording and location of the information.

    a.   True
    b.   False

1.   The types of ownership are important for you to understand so that you may:

2.   Name the _____ unities that may exist in this type of ownership.

3.   Name three forms of this type of tenancy.

4.   Name five special entity or individual owners whose interests in real property may require special items of scrutiny on the part of the abstractor.

5.   Sole ownership may be held by

_____
_____
_____
_____
_____
_____

6.   Tenancy by Severalty is also known as _____ _____and means
      that the ownership of a property is

_____
_____
_____
_____
_____
_____

7.   Concurrent ownership is ownership held by _____ or more individuals.

8.   The term _____ refers to the administration of the property and
      interest of a _____ or _____ individual.

9.   A title company may occasionally rely on either an _____ or
      _____ agreement for the elimination of the marital rights of a
      spouse.

10.   Any action taken by _____ interested owner will affect the title to the
      _____ you are researching

11.   Tenancy by Severalty means there are

      a.   Two owners
      b.   Many Owners
      c.   One Owner
      d.   All of the above

12. Concurrent owners share

   a. The property
   b. Unity
   c. Ownership interest
   d. All of the above

13. Tenancy in common occurs

   a. Without the right of survivorship
   b. When ownership is held by two or more individuals
   c. With the unity of possession
   d. All of the above

14. Any owner of a property may

   a. Incur liens
   b. Convey interest
   c. Create a condemnation
   d. All of the above

15. An Ante nuptial agreement

   a. Does not affect property ownership
   b. Does not affect disposition of property
   c. Does not affect the research process
   d. None of the above

16. Any entity transferring property

   a. Must have legal right to hold title to real property
   b. May be empowered by escheat to transfer property
   c. Must advertise the transfer
   d. All of the above

1.   Name the two types of liens you will encounter during your search and describe them.

2.   Name four types of judgments you may encounter in your search process.

3.   A mortgage lien is created when:

4.   A foreclosure proceeding is

5. Liens are prioritized by _____ and this order dictates that

_____
_____
_____
_____
_____
_____

6. A _____ _____ goes against an individual and attaches to all of the _____ _____ of that individual within the county.

7. A _____ _____ goes against a specific property.

8. The lien that always comes first in the order of priority regardless of the time is the _____ _____.

9. If you locate a judgment lien with regard to the property you are searching, you should research to determine if the judgment has been _____.

10. The _____ _____ law gives anyone that has furnished _____ or _____ for the improvement of a parcel of land the right to place a lien against the improvements and the land.

11. What type of lien is created against a property when an owner uses it as collateral to borrower money?

    a. General Lien
    b. Voluntary Lien
    c. Involuntary Lien
    d. All of the above

12. A general lien goes against an individual and does not impact real property

    a. True
    b. False

13. Which of the following best describes a real estate property tax lien?

   a. Voluntary Lien
   b. General Lien
   c. Specific Lien
   d. All of the above

14. A property tax lien can be attached to multiple properties.

   a. True
   b. False

15. When a property is sold by order of the court it is termed a

   a. Judgment Lien
   b. Foreclosure
   c. Escheat
   d. All of the above

16. Liens may be imposed against

   a. Fixtures
   b. Improvements
   c. Real Property
   d. All of the above

17. Which type of sale gives the purchaser a lien against the property for the taxes, assessed fees and interest owing from unpaid real estate tax assessments?

   a. Foreclosure Sale
   b. Judicial Sale
   c. Subject To Sale
   d. None of the above

18. Tax liens are similar to mechanics liens and voluntary liens in that they are recorded and paid in order of priority.

   a. True
   b. False

Name:
Real Estate Title Search Abstractor
Chapter 6 – Deeds Review Questions
Score:
Instructor:

1.   Explain the purpose of a deed.

2.   What is considered the best deed a buyer can obtain from a seller?

3.   What does a grant deed warrant?

4.   What does a bargain and sale deed warrant?

5.   What is the purpose of a correction deed?

_____
_____
_____
_____
_____

6.   The physical transfer of a deed before the death of the grantor is known as

_____
_____
_____
_____
_____

7.   List five of the most common covenants you may find in a deed of transfer.

_____
_____
_____
_____
_____

8.   Explain the purpose of an exception in a deed.

_____
_____
_____
_____
_____

9.   The basic _____ and _____ deed contains no covenants and only the minimal essentials of the deed.

10. Each _____ on the deed and the _____ _____,
inclusions and type of deed within the public records of the property you are researching
will affect the rights of any future owner of that property.

11. A general warranty deed is the lowest form of deed.

    a. True
    b. False

12. A quitclaim deed

    a. contains no warranties
    b. contains no covenants
    c. does not promise the seller even holds interest in the property
    d. all of the above

13. A cession deed is a form of

    a. General Warranty Deed
    b. Quitclaim Deed
    c. Guardians Deed
    d. None of the above

14. Reservations in the deed are made in favor of

    a.   the Government
    b.   the Grantee
    c.   the Grantor
    d.   the Taxing Authority

15. A deed restriction may limit

    a.   the action of a lender
    b.   the action of the owner
    c.   the action of an investor
    d.   all of the above

16.   The abstractor should review all documents and note any exception, restriction or other matter that may limit the rights of an owner.

        True
        False

Name:
Real Estate Title Search Abstractor
Chapter 7 – Understanding Contracts Review Questions
Score:
Instructor:

1.   What does a real estate sales contract outline?

2.   List five common alternate names you might encounter for a real estate sales contract.

3.   List three alternate names commonly used for the contract for deed.

4.   Under a contract for deed who holds legal title to the property?

5.   What does the buyer gain under a contract for deed?

6.   Who may assign their interest in the property under a contract for deed?

7.   Explain the purpose of an option to purchase.

8.   What three possible avenues must you explore when you discover an option to purchase in the chain of title?

9.   Unless an issue arises, deeds are the only legal documents you must review in the title search process.

     a.   True
     b.   False

10. Equitable title is

   a. a title that is fair and provides an even interest to all parties
   b. an interest created between the recording of the sales agreement and the deed
   c. a synonym for the abstract of title
   d. none of the above

11. The status of all sales contracts should be researched.

   a. True
   b. False

12. You can confirm that a sales contract was terminated by locating

   a. proof of the sale and acquisition by the buyer named
   b. a judicial decree terminating the contract
   c. a recording instrument terminating the contract
   d. any of the above

13. Another name you may locate for a contact for deed is

   a. installment land contract
   b. acquisition contract
   c. purchaser option
   d. any of the above

14. When a contract for deed exists, you should note

   a. the existence of the contract
   b. the parties to the contract
   c. the condition of the contract
   d. all of the above

15. If a contract that has not been terminated exists in record, options may include

    a. obtaining a judicial decree
    b. obtaining a seller declaration of forfeiture
    c. obtaining an executed release from the buyer
    d. any of the above

16. An option may be removed from exception requirements if

    a. the option has expired
    b. the underwriter deems the risk at a low level
    c. the option holder has died
    d. any of the above

1.   How is constructive notice given?

2.   Actual notice is the knowledge that one has actually gained based on what is:

3.   When completing an abstract of title you will begin with:

4.   What can be found on a tract index page?

5.   How are grantor indexes arranged:

6.   Explain the concept of a chain of title.

7.   What action will you take if you discover a break (missing item) within the chain of title?

8.   Constructive notice is accomplished by the _____ of a document at the county recorder office.

9.   The simplest indexes to use are the_____ _____.

10.   The documents presented for recording will be _____ and the copies will be placed in the _____ with indexes.

        The book and index _____ will be noted on the _____.

11. Constructive notice is not accomplished by

    a. Visibly occupying the property
    b. Recording a document within public record
    c. Public notice within the mandated advertising media
    d. All of the above

12. Inquiry notice is the responsibility of

    a. The purchaser of a property
    b. The owner of a property
    c. The taxing authority
    d. All of the above

13. Actual notice is gained by what is

    a. Observed
    b. Heard
    c. Seen
    d. All of the above

14. A tract index allocates

    a. One page to a parcel or land group
    b. One page to each property owner
    c. One page to each assessor's map
    d. All of the above

15. A Grantor Index are formatted

    a. As one page per grantor
    b. Alphabetically
    c. Chronologically
    d. All of the above

Name:
Real Estate Title Search Abstractor
Chapter 9 – The Title Exam Review
Questions
Score:
Instructor:

1.   What basic items does the title exam report?

2.   A chain of title is a compilation of what?

3.   Provide four obvious breaks in the chain of title you may encounter.

4.   Provide three common defects in title you might encounter during your search.

5.	Name four additional records you might refer to during your research beyond the basic indexes and maps.

6.	Fill in the recorded items the abstract must recite in chronological order.

7.	Provide two reasons that an abstract might contain faulty data without the responsibility being the abstractors.

8.	What protection does title insurance offer?

9.	The chain is arranged _____ from the initial government patent or original source of the title to the present _____.

10. The chain of title is complete when all events are _____ from the original source of title to the present owner. If there is a _____ link, the current owner does not have _____ title to the property.

11. A chain of title is a record that links all previous lenders in order of priority.

   a. True
   b. False

12. To research a chain of title you should all review

   a. linkage of all owners from the original land grant to today
   b. all matters or record that pertain to the property of research
   c. any breaks in the chain of title that appear
   d. all of the above

13. In all cases, the chain of title will begin with the original government land grant to a company.

   a. True
   b. False

14. Your search function will be contained only to those documents located within the recorder's office.

   a. True
   b. False

15. A break in the chain of title may occur as a result of

   a. a judicial determination not filed for record
   b. insufficient deeds of conveyance
   c. missing deeds or other documents
   d. all of the above

16. When a break in the chain of title exists, it should be

    a.   specifically excepted in the records
    b.   remedied through the proper procedures
    c.   noted and the next link in the chain researched
    d.   any of the above

17. A defect in the title might be a result of the lack of termination of a

    a.   marriage
    b.   judgment
    c.   lien
    d.   any of the above

18. Prior to considering an abstract complete, you must research

    a.   Local Tax Rolls
    b.   Lis Pendens Indexes
    c.   Mechanic's Liens
    d.   All of the above

19. If a defect exists, your responsibility is to note the applicable data within your report so the underwriter may determine the handling of the defect.

    a.   True
    b.   False

20. If a defect exists, you should

    a.   determine if the defect still exists and make the proper notation
    b.   detail any alterations that occurred with regard to the defect
    c.   note the method, time and processes that eliminated the defect
    d.   all of the above

21.   An abstract of title will include

       a.   a historical summary of the chain of title
       b.   the status of any defects that exist in the chain of title
       c.   a comprehensive explanation of any item of issue in the chain of title
       d.   all of the above

22.   The abstractor will

       a.   summarize each document located within the record
       b.   note the book and page of each document located within the record
       c.   note the date of each document entered into record
       d.   all of the above

23.   Individuals preparing the abstract are liable for mistakes they make during the research
       process.

       a.   True
       b.   False

24.   At times, mistakes in the preparation of the abstract may not be the fault of the
       abstractor conducting the search.

       a.   True
       b.   False

25.   Title insurance is designed to protect

       a.   issues that come to light after the completion of the abstract
       b.   the abstractor
       c.   the insurance holder
       d.   all of the above

Name:
Real Estate Title Search
Chapter 9 – Title Insurance Review Questions
Score:
Instructor:

1.   How does title insurance differ from other forms of insurance?

2.   What is a quiet title suit?

3.   What is a certificate of title?

4.   Name the four items that must be present for the issuance of title insurance.

5. What are the components of a title insurance policy?

6. What is the purpose of affirmative insurance?

7. What is the major issue that arises with belated coverage causing additional scrutiny?

8. The title commitment will be _____ with the same date and time that you noted as the _____ date and time for your abstracting summery

9. Title commitment, commitment, or title binder refers to the _____ document _____ by the title company that provides formal contract to _____ the title.

10. The _____ is the written declaration of a statement of _____ that is made voluntarily and sworn to or affirmed before some person legally _____ to administer an oath or affirmation.

11. The title insurance process begins with

    a.   the title underwriter examining the file to determine suitability to the companies guidelines
    b.   the title attorney issuing an opinion as to the owner's rights to be transferred
    c.   the title abstractor examining public records to determine the status of the title
    d.   none of the above

12. The title exam includes

    a.   a review of the chain of title
    b.   specifics of any defects encountered during research
    c.   information regarding the status of any defects encountered
    d.   all of the above

13. Title insurance insures against future occurrences rather than past events

    a.   True
    b.   False

14. The date and time you completed the abstract must be noted because

    a.   additional issues may arise following your abstract report
    b.   you must confirm the length of the search term
    c.   the insurance premiums will be based upon the time of your search
    d.   none of the above

15. Title insurance issuance will be based on

    a.   the status of the purchaser
    b.   the completion of a search and exam of public records
    c.   the lender's assessment of borrower suitability
    d.   all of the above

16. Schedule B of the title commitment will contain

    a. the policies and commitment coverage's
    b. the matters that affect the land as detailed in the legal description
    c. general, standard, and special exceptions to coverage
    d. all of the above

17. When you discover a defect in the title insurance cannot be issued

    a. True
    b. False

18. Affirmative insurance is also termed

    a. positive insurance
    b. insuring over
    c. title insurance
    d. none of the above

Section

3

Self-Test Answer Keys

1.   A title search must have the ability to:

       Carefully and accurately, search public records

       Review and establish a chain of title

       Determine any defects to the title that may exist

       Document the status of these defects

2.   Advanced abstracting duties might include:

       The creation of the title commitment

       The underwriting of specific issues on the property

       The issuance of title policies that contain title bulletins and exceptions

3.   Give the three characteristics most frequently sought in a title abstractor:

       A methodical approach to the tasks at hand

       The ability to bring high levels of focus to your work

       provide careful research

       A dedication to the concise completion of each task

4.   Give the three most common career choices for a newly trained title abstractor:

Full-time employment with a title or closing company

Contract abstractor performing functions for various businesses

Self-employed abstractor working to complete title search activities for individuals and businesses outside of the normal mortgage-lending sphere

5.   The primary concern of a title abstractor is:

The abstractor must determine how events that have occurred during the chain of title, often termed defects, effect the ability of the current owner of real property to transfer a full bundle of rights to the new purchaser

6.   Your abstract of title will include activities that affect the title from:

The date of the original land grant on the property through the last abstract certificate issued on that property

7.   The primary duty of a title abstractor is:

The abstractor will determine the rights and interests in the land and the ability of these rights to be transferred.

8.   What two specific determinations will be made based upon your abstracting report?

If the individual representing himself or herself as the owner of the property actually has the legal right to transfer the property in question

What if any defects exist on the title of the property being researched including those defects brought against the current or past owner that directly impact the clarity of the title

9.   <u>Title companies</u> and <u>insurance commitments</u> base their entire process around the work that you perform during your research

10.   The career of real estate title abstractor is <u>essential</u> to the <u>operation</u> of the real estate title insurance and closing industries and as such requires <u>careful</u>, <u>detail oriented</u>, and <u>methodical</u> practices on your part.

11.   D

12.   D

13.   C

14.   D

15.   B

1.   What are the three rights that may be transferred or severed from the transfer of land?

        Surface rights
        Sub-surface rights – including mineral rights
        Air rights

2.   Name the four standards to be applied when determining if an item is considered a fixture:

        The intention of the parties in the transaction
        An agreement between the parties in the transaction
        The manner in which the item is attached to the real property
        The item itself and its adaptation to the real estate

3.   Explain a reason that a fixture might not be insurable as part of the title commitment even when the real property contains no liens:

        A built in appliance for which outside financing has been obtained using the appliance as security may not be insured as part of the lending process. This would be true although the fixture meets the four criteria unless the lien against the appliance is paid in full prior to the real property transfer. The appliance is technically still owned in part or in whole by the finance company.

4.   The term severance when applied to real property rights and interests means:

        to sever or remove a right or interest from the overall bundle of rights which will be transferred

5.   Real property <u>surface</u> rights include the <u>improvements</u> that exist and area actually <u>affixed</u> to the surface of the land.

6.   A <u>fixture</u> is a piece of personal property that has been <u>affixed</u>, <u>installed</u> or <u>permanently attached</u> to a parcel of land or the structures on the land.

7.   Crops are also known as <u>fructus</u> <u>industrias</u> or <u>fruits</u> of <u>industry</u>.

8.   A property's <u>value</u> is effected its ability to transfer <u>full rights</u> to the new purchaser.

9.   Sub-surface resources are subject to the same rights of <u>ownership</u> as any <u>other</u> portion of the land.

10.   If an item is classified as <u>personal property,</u> it will not be included in the sale of real property.

11.   D

12.   A

13.   B

14.   A

15.   C

16.   A

17.   D

18.   A

19.   A

20.   A

1.   Name the methods of land descriptions you will encounter during the title search process.

        Informal Reference
        Metes and Bounds
        Rectangular Survey
        Recorded Plat
        Assessor's Parcel Number
        Referral to another document
        State Referral Method
        Survey

2.   The method that provides land description through street numbers and place names is known as INFORMAL REFERENCE and the primary advantage of this method of description is:

        It is easily understood.

3.   Direction is shown as:

        Degrees – 360 in a circle
        Minutes – 60 minutes in a degree
        Seconds – 60 seconds in minute

4.   The point where a parcel survey begins is frequently termed the:

        Point of beginning

5.   The rectangular survey system is also termed:

        Government Survey
        US Public Land Survey

6.   What method of surveying is used to describe the most landmass in the United States?

        Rectangular Survey Method

7.   A check or quadrangle contains how many miles?

       24 mile x 24 mile area

8.   Define a survey:

       A survey is defined as the process of measuring land to determine its exact area.

9.   Who sets the standards and requirements for surveyors in the United States?

       The American Land Title Association
       The American Congress of Surveying and Mapping

10.   The <u>metes and bounds</u> method begins at a <u>monument</u>, which is a permanent reference mark.

11.   Distance and direction is another term for <u>metes and bounds surveying</u>.

12.   It is customary to describe a parcel by going <u>clockwise</u>.

13.   Latitude lines run <u>east-west</u> while longitude lines run <u>north-south</u>.

14.   Another term for the lot-block-tract system is the <u>recorded plat</u>.

15.   The <u>assessor's parcel number</u> is a number assigned by the tax assessor to aid in tax collection.

16.   A
17.   C
18.   B
19.   A
20.   C
21.   B
22.   D
23.   C
24.   C
25.   A

1.   All access points relating to the property being researched should:

       Be included in your abstract report with full details regarding the conveyance or condemnation of the access.

2.   Physical access is:

       The actual ability to use an access point

       Legal access is:

       The legal ability to use an access point

3.   When you begin your research activity with regard to access it is best to:

       Consider every property landlocked until you have proven otherwise by finding conveyance of access that is undisputed.

4.   Define accretion

       The process by which a piece of land is increased or extended by the gradual deposit of soil as a result of the action of a river, stream, lake, pond or mass of tidal waters that border the property.

5.   List the three items you must specifically research in relationship to beach property.

       Whether the wet sand area is considered to be held by the government in trust

       Whether the title to the wet sand area is held for the benefit of the public

       Whether the public has acquired access to the use of any part of the beach area or access to the beach area through adverse use or local custom

6.   A riparian right is a right that occurs when a property borders a _river_ or _stream_.

7.   A littoral right is a right that occurs when a property borders a _sea_ OR _lake_.

9.   The <u>DOCTRINE</u> OF _prior appropriation_ may come into effect that allows the first landowner that diverts water for his use to continue this diversion although it is not fair to other landowners.

10.   A common <u>appurtenance</u> would be an <u>easement</u> or right-of-way that was gained for that particular parcel of land.

11.   C

12.   D

13.   A

14.   A

15.   D

16.   A

17.   B

18.   B

19.   B

20.   B

1.   Name the two parties who obtain rights to property:

       The government and the individual or entity owner

2.   Define the term encumbrance.

       An encumbrance is any claim, right, lien, estate or liability that limits the fee simple title to a property.

3.   Explain the use of inheritance tax.

       Inheritance tax is paid when a decedent receives property at the time of the death of a grantor.

4.   Explain the use of estate tax.

       Estate tax is the tax imposed on the right to transmit a piece of property upon death or in contemplation of death.

5.   The system of governing estates in the US most closely resembles the <u>Allodial</u> <u>system</u>.

6.   The highest and most complete form of estate ownership is the <u>freehold</u> <u>estate</u>, which is typically transferred using a <u>fee simple transfer</u>.

7.   A life estate provides a <u>lifelong right</u> to use and occupy and when it ends, the estate reverts to the original grantor who is also known as the <u>reversionary</u>.

8.   The concept of real estate ownership can be easiest understood when you view ownership as a <u>bundle of rights </u>or collection of rights to ownership.

9.   The abstract report is specifically concerned with rights that are <u>granted</u> as well as rights that are <u>limited</u> in a real estate transfer.

10.   If a person dies without a will or having disposed of their property, the laws of intestacy property will come into effect. This is also known as the <u>statutes of descent and distribution</u>.

11.   A

12.   C

13.   B

14.   D

15.   D

16.   B

17.   B

18.   B

19.   B

20.   D

21.   D

22.   B

1.   The term bundle of rights refers to:

        The level of interest one has in real property can be described as the collective rights of ownership interest in a property.

2.   Name four rights retained by the government.

        Taxation
        Eminent Domain
        Police Power
        Escheat

3.   Explain how a deed restriction or <u>reservation in deed</u> may be enforced.

        A deed restriction can be enforced through the civil courts through court action brought by any party who is affected by the restriction.

4.   Give the explanation for an easement by prescription:

        The open, continuous, notorious and hostile use of the property of another for a proscribed period.

5.   The government right of <u>police power</u> is imposed to protect the health, <u>safety and general welfare</u> of the public.

6.   An example of government <u>easement by condemnation</u> occurs when the government is acting to control a flood area and runs a drainage pipe <u>over</u> or <u>under</u> an owner's property.

7.   The non-payment of <u>property taxes</u> may result in the government seizure of property resulting in the loss of an owner's interest. This occurs in an attempt to gain the needed revenue for specific operations.

8.   The process of <u>eminent domain</u> is the taking of a piece of private property for <u>public use</u>.

9.   If an individual loses the ability to enjoy full use of his property through the actions of another, he may bring an <u>inverse condemnation</u> suit.

10.   An easement grants the right to <u>come through</u> a certain portion of a privately owned property.

11.   B

12.   B

13.   A

14.   C

15.   D

16.   C

17.   B

18.   D

19.   A

20.   B

Name:
Real Estate Title Search Abstractor
Chapter 4 – Forms of Ownership Review Questions Answer Key
Score:
Instructor:

1.   The types of ownership are important for you to understand so that you may:

       Ensure that you have a full understanding of all potential owners who may have
       obtained an interest to a piece of real property so that you may research any action each
       owner might have taken that has an impact on the title condition.

2.   Name the <u>five</u> unities that may exist in this type of ownership.

       Unity of Time
       Unity of Title
       Unity of Possession
       Unity of Interest
       Unity of Person

3.   Name three forms of this type of tenancy.

       Tenancy by the entirety
       Joint tenancy
       Tenancy in common

4.   Name five special entity or individual owners whose interests in real property may
       require special items of scrutiny on the part of the abstractor.

       Business Trusts
       Banks or Savings Institutions
       Credit Unions
       Corporations
       Aliens
       Convicts
       Government Entities

5.   Sole ownership may be held by

       An individual
       Married couples
       Corporations considered a single entity

6. Tenancy by Severalty is also known as <u>sole ownership</u> and means that the ownership of a property is

    CUT OFF FROM OTHER INDIVIDUALS AND THE NAMED INDIVIDUAL OWNS THE PROPERTY ALONE.

7. Concurrent ownership is ownership held by <u>tow</u> or more individuals.

8. The term <u>guardianship</u> refers to the administration of the property and interest of a <u>minor</u> or <u>incompetent</u> individual.

9. A title company may occasionally rely on either an <u>ante nuptial</u> or <u>prenuptial</u> agreement for the elimination of the marital rights of a spouse.

10. Any action taken by <u>any</u> interested owner will affect the title to the <u>property</u> you are researching.

11. C

12. D

13. D

14. D

15. D

16. A

1. Name the two types of liens you will encounter during your search and describe them.

   Voluntary lien created when a property owner voluntarily creates a lien against a property.

   Involuntary lien created by the operation or enforcement of the law.

2. Name four types of judgments you may encounter in your search process.

   Declaratory Judgment
   Money Judgment
   Judgment in Rem
   Federal Judgment
   Foreign Judgment
   Judgment in Personam
   Dormant Judgment

3. A mortgage lien is created when:

   A property is offered by the owner as security for the repayment of a mortgage debt.

4. A foreclosure proceeding is

   A legal procedure where the mortgagor or other lien holder obtains the real estate securing a debt that has fallen into default for the purpose of obtaining the funds owed on that debt.

5. Liens are prioritized by <u>time</u> and this order dictates that

   The first lien filed receives a higher priority than the later liens filed except those liens that usurp the priority of time.

6. A <u>general lien</u> goes against an individual and attaches to all of the <u>real property</u> of that individual within the county.

7.	A <u>specific lien</u> goes against a specific property.

8.	The lien that always comes first in the order of priority regardless of the time is the <u>tax lien</u>.

9.	If you locate a judgment lien with regard to the property you are searching, you should research to determine if the judgment has been <u>terminated</u>.

10.	The <u>mechanic's lien law</u> gives anyone that has furnished <u>labor</u> or <u>materials</u> for the improvement of a parcel of land the right to place a lien against the improvements and the land.

11.	B

12.	B

13.	C

14.	B

15.	B

16.	D

17.	D

18.	B

Name:
Real Estate Title Search Abstractor
Chapter 6 – Deeds Review Questions Answer Key
Score:
Instructor:

1.   Explain the purpose of a deed.

        A deed conveys or transfers ownership interests in land from one person or entity to
        another.

2.   What is considered the best deed a buyer can obtain from a seller?

        General Warranty Deed

3.   What does a grant deed warrant?

        The seller who provides a grant-deed warrant only the time that particular owner had
        possession of the title.

4.   What does a bargain and sale deed warrant?

        The bargain and sale deed contains no warranties and covenants. When using this type
        of deed the seller only implies that he owns the property described in the deed with no
        guarantee as to the condition of the title or the right to transfer the property.

5.   What is the purpose of a correction deed?

        A correction deed is used to correct an error in a previously executed and delivered
        deed.

6.   The physical transfer of a deed before the death of the grantor is known as

        Actual delivery

7.   List five of the most common covenants you may find in a deed of transfer.

       Covenant of Seizin
       Covenant of Enjoyment
       Covenant against Encumbrances
       Covenant of Further Assurance
       Covenant of Right to Convey
       Covenant of Non-Claim

8.   Explain the purpose of an exception in a deed.

       An exception is included to withhold or exclude part of the estate or land being conveyed from the transfer.

9.   The basic _bargain_ and _sale_ deed contains no covenants and only the minimal essentials of the deed.

10.   Each _entry_ on the deed and the _specific_ _wording_, inclusions and type of deed within the public records of the property you are researching will affect the rights of any future owner of that property.

11.   B

12.   D

13.   B

14.   C

15.   D

16.   A

1.   What does a real estate sales contract outline?

        All of the terms and conditions of the sale between a seller and a buyer.

2.   List five common alternate names you might encounter for a real estate sales contract.

        Offer to purchase
        Option to buy or sell
        Sales Agreement
        Contract for the purchase of real estate
        Contract for deed

3.   List three alternate names commonly used for the contract for deed.

        Land Contract
        Article of Agreement
        Installment Land Contract

4.   Under a contract for deed who holds legal title to the property?

        The seller

5.   What does the buyer gain under a contract for deed?

        Possession of the property and equitable title

6.   Who may assign their interest in the property under a contract for deed?

        Both parties may assign their interest in the property.

7.   Explain the purpose of an option to purchase.

        An option to purchase real property is a contract that allows the right to purchase the property to a specific individual at a specific price and within a specific time frame.

8. What three possible avenues must you explore when you discover an option to purchase in the chain of title?

   Establish that the option conveyed has expired in time.

   Establish that an additional document was created terminating the option.

   Generate the information that will be needed by the title underwriter to generate an exception regarding this option.

9. B

10. D

11. A

12. D

13. A

14. D

15. D

16. D

1.   How is constructive notice given?

Through the recording of a document at the county recorder office.

2.   Actual notice is the knowledge that one has actually gained based on what is:

Seen
Heard
Read
Observed
Witnessed

3.   When completing an abstract of title you will begin with:

the most recently recorded document and then work backward through the records until you reach the original land grant.

4.   What can be found on a tract index page?

A list of all recorded deeds, mortgages and other documents related to a particular parcel.

5.   How are grantor indexes arranged:

All grantors named in each document for a record year are listed in alphabetical order and placed in the grantor index.

6.   Explain the concept of a chain of title.

A chain of title can be viewed as a group of links moving backward through time from the most recent transaction to the original land grant. If a link in the chain is broken or missing then the chain is not complete.

7.   What action will you take if you discover a break (missing item) within the chain of title?

     You will research all possible document storage locations to find the missing piece of information enabling you to mend the break in the chain. If the applicable information is not available, you will note all applicable details and refer the issue to the title underwriter assigned to the file.

8.   Constructive notice is accomplished by the <u>recording</u> of a document at the county recorder office.

9.   The simplest indexes to use are the <u>tract indexes</u>.

10. The documents presented for recording will be <u>photocopied</u> and the copies will be placed in the <u>book</u> with indexes.

     The book and index <u>pages</u> will be noted on the <u>document</u>.

11. D

12. A

13. D

14. A

15. D

1.   What basic items does the title exam report?

        Chain of Title
        Breaks in the Chain of Title
        Defects in Title
        Status of Defects

2.   A chain of title is a compilation of what?

        All real estate instruments and other matters of record that effect the title of a particular piece of land.

3.   Provide four obvious breaks in the chain of title you may encounter.

        Missing deeds of conveyance

        Insufficient deeds of conveyance or other instruments

        Lack of adequate judicial proceedings

        Judicial determinations that are not filed for record at the office designated by statute

        Factual or non-judicial information that was not filed for record at the office designated by statute

        Other reasons as statutorily proscribed

4.   Provide three common defects in title you might encounter during your search.

        Mortgages

        Liens

        Judgments

        Easements

        Lawsuits

Active contracts

5. Name four additional records you might refer to during your research beyond the basic indexes and maps.

    Birth records

    Marriage records

    Divorce records

    Adoption records

    Probate court records

    Military files

    Federal tax lien logs

    Assessment Records

6. Fill in the recorded items the abstract must recite in chronological order.

    Conveyances

    Easements

    Mortgages

    Wills

    Tax liens

    Agreements

    Judgments

    Pending lawsuits

    Marriages

    Divorces

    Deaths

7.   Provide two reasons that an abstract might contain faulty data without the responsibility being the abstractors.

A married person represents himself on the deed, as a single person the deed may be invalidated.

A minor might have executed the deed causing potential validity questions.

An incompetent person may have executed the deed causing the validity of the deed to be called into question.

The deed may contain erroneous descriptions.

8.   What protection does title insurance offer?

Title insurance protects against losses that may arise from title defects that are not the fault of the abstractor and from title defects that were not located by the abstractor during the examination.

9.   The chain is arranged <u>consecutively</u> from the initial government patent or original source of the title to the present <u>titleholder</u>.

10.   The chain of title is complete when all events are <u>documented</u> from the original source of title to the present owner. If there is a <u>missing link</u>, the current owner does not have <u>valid</u> title to the property.

11.   B
12.   D
13.   B
14.   B
15.   D
16.   B
17.   D
18.   D
19.   A
20.   D
21.   D
22.   D

23. A

24. B

25. D

1.   How does title insurance differ from other forms of insurance?

        Title insurance insures against occurrences that occurred from the date the covered
        individual secured the insurance into the past while typical insurance provides coverage
        against events that may occur in the future.

2.   What is a quiet title suit?

        A quiet title suit is a court ordered hearing to determine land ownership.

3.   What is a certificate of title?

        A certificate of title is an opinion issued by an attorney detailing who rightfully owns a
        piece of land.

4.   Name the four items that must be present for the issuance of title insurance.

        A complete search of public records
        A valid title commitment
        A bona fide purchaser
        Full disclosure of all matters that affect the property

5.   What are the components of a title insurance policy?

        Commitment
        Schedules A and B
        Affidavits
        Releases
        Exceptions
        Acknowledgments
        Validation of Acknowledgements
        Endorsements

6.   What is the purpose of affirmative insurance?

        To insure over a specific defect lien, encumbrance or interest that affects the title.

7.   What is the major issue that arises with belated coverage causing additional   scrutiny?

        The purchaser in possession of the property is not a bone fide purchaser. Any request at
        such a late time is suspect, causing one to consider that the owner may have gained
        knowledge of some defect he is now attempting to gain insurance coverage to offset.

8.   The title commitment will be dated with the same date and time that you noted as the
        completion date and time for your abstracting summery

9.   Title commitment, commitment, or title binder refers to the binding document issued by
        the title company that provides formal contract to insure the title.

10.   The affidavit is the written declaration of a statement of fact that is made voluntarily and
        sworn to or affirmed before some person legally authorized to administer an oath or
        affirmation.

11.   C

12.   D

13.   B

14.   A

15.   B

16.   C

17.   B

18.   C

Abstracting Review Forms

SAMPLE ABSTRACTOR SUMMARY

Date: _____ Client: _____

Search Purpose/Notes: _____

Property Street Address: _____

Map Book Number: _____ Map Parcel Number: _____ Taxes: $_____/_____Status: _____

Grantor: _____ Grantee: _____

Deed Book Volume: _____ Page Number: _____ Date: _____ Deed Type: _____

Legal Description: _____

_____

_____

Access: _____

Easements/Restrictions/Other Matters: _____

_____

Mortgage: _____ Satisfied: Y/N   Book / Page: _____/_____

Borrower(s) Name: _____

Notes: _____

Liens/Judgments/Other Matters: _____

Notes: _____

_____

_____

_____

_____

_____

_____

The following quick list will assist you in locating the necessary records to complete the abstract of the title, locate any defects that exist and determine the status of any defects that exist within the chain of the title you are researching.

- **Grantee/Grantor Indexes**

  ➢ Current Property Owner

  This entry will be located in the index for the year that the current owner obtained his interest in the property.

  The index will provide a reference to the book and page where the deed of conveyance by which he took title to the property is recorded.

  ➢ Previous Owner

  A review of the deed of conveyance will provide you with the name of the owner from whom the current owner took possession. You will then work backward through the previous indexes to locate the entry that indicates the document by which this previous owner took ownership interest.

  By continuing this process backward through all deeds of conveyance, you will construct the chain of title.

- **Grantor / Grantee Index / Mortgagee Index**

  ➢ Real property transfer documents

  ➢ Liens

  ➢ Judgments

  ➢ Assignments

  ➢ Power of attorney

  ➢ Additional Contracts

  ➢ Other matters pertaining to the specific title you are researching

Some states will place mortgages within the general grantor and grantee indexes, while others will have ea separate index that details only mortgage instruments. You must determine the method employed in the state where you will conduct your research.

If a mortgage is located within the public records, the applicable records will provide you with the status of the mortgage. The mortgage may be satisfied, release or active. If a mortgage is released and satisfied, the recorder's office will place a note on the margin of the recorded mortgage instrument indicating the book and page where the release is located.

- **Judgment Rolls, Lis Pendens Index, General Execution Docket**

  ➢ General Liens

  ➢ Specific Liens

  ➢ Pending Lawsuits

A defect on the title may exist in the form of a judgment or pending lawsuits may affect the transfer of ownership interest. You can locate information pertaining to judgments within the Judgment Rolls and relating to pending lawsuits within the Lis Pendens Index.

- **Assessor's Records / Ad Valorem Docket**

  ➢ Current property taxes

  ➢ Delinquent Taxes

  ➢ Special Assessments

  ➢ Tax Liens

  ➢ Current owner name and address

- **County map records, survey reports and plat maps**

  ➤ Legal Description

  ➤ Property size

  ➤ Boundary specifics

  ➤ Boundary Line Issues or Agreements

  ➤ Appurtenances

  ➤ Easements

  ➤ Right of Ways

  ➤ Right of Access

  ➤ Quality of Access

  ➤ Abutting or adjoining property and roads

  ➤ Measurements

  ➤ Improvements

  ➤ Easements

  ➤ Utilities

  ➤ Features

  ➤ Accretion or Erosion that alters the land description

  ➤ Littoral, riparian, beach rights

  ➤ Flood Plain Designation

- **Tract Index**

  - Real property transfer documents

  - Liens

  - Judgments

  - Assignments

  - Power of attorney

  - Additional Contracts

  - Other matters pertaining to the specific title you are researching

- **Civil court records**

  - Foreclosure actions

  - Legal Proceedings against a property owner

  - Other legal proceedings

- **Divorce Records**

  - To locate the removal of a property owner's interest through a divorce decree

- **Marriage Records**

  - To determine the addition of a potential property owner through a marriage

- **Probate court records**

  ➤ Additional interest transfers

  ➤ Status of inheritance and estate tax payments

- **State and Federal tax lien logs**

To aid in the determination of whether any federal or state liens against a property owner may have attached to the property

Land Contract

This Agreement is made and entered into by and between _____ (seller), whose address is,_____

hereinafter called the Vendor and _____ (buyer)

whose address is _____

hereinafter called the Vendee.

Witnesseth: The Vendor, for himself, his heirs and assigns, does hereby agree to sell to the Vendee, their heirs and assigns, the following real estate commonly known as: _____ and further described; as _____together with all appurtenances, rights, privileges, easements, and all buildings and fixtures in their present condition located upon said property.

1.   CONTRACT PRICE METHOD OF PAYMENT, INTEREST RATE:

   In consideration whereof, the Vendee agrees to purchase the above-described property for the sum of _____
   Dollars ($_____), payable as follows:

   The sum of $_____ as initial consideration at the time of execution of the within Land Contract, the receipt of which is hereby acknowledged, leaving a principal balance owed by Vendee of $_____ together with interest on the unpaid balance payable in consecutive monthly installments of $_____ beginning on the _____ day of _____20____, and on the _____ day of each and every month thereafter until said balance and interest is paid in full, or until the _____ day of _____ 20_____ at which time the entire remaining balance plus accrued interest shall become due and payable.

   The interest on the unpaid balance due hereon shall be (_____ %) percent annum computed monthly, in accordance with a month amortization schedule during the life of this agreement.

   Payments shall be credited first to the interest. The remainder to the principal or other sums due Vendor. The total amount of this obligation, both principal and interest, unpaid after making any such application of payments as herein receipted shall be the interest bearing principal amount of this obligation for the next succeeding interest computation period. If any payment is not received within _____ (_____) days of payment date, there shall be a late charge of (_____%) percent assessed.

The Vendees may pay the entire purchase price on this contract without prepayment penalty. The monthly installments shall be payable as directed by the Vendor herein.

2. ENCUMBRANCES:

Said real estate is presently subject to a mortgage with_____
and the Vendor shall not place any additional mortgage on the premises without the prior written permission of the Vendees. To protect Vendee's interests.
Vendee may elect at any time to pay any sums due hereunder directly to the mortgagee, and any amounts remaining to the Vendor.
Vendor understands that this transaction may permit the mortgagee to exercise their right to accelerate the loan and to call the remaining balance due. In any such event, the Vendor agrees to hold Vendee harmless and in no way liable for any damage to Vendor because of such action. Vendor initials _____.

3. EVIDENCE OF TITLE:

The Vendor shall be required to provide an abstract or guarantee of title, statement of title, title insurance, or such other evidence of title to Vendee's satisfaction.

4. RECORDING OF CONTRACT:

The Vendor shall permit a copy of this contract to be recorded in the _____County Recorder's Office at Vendee's discretion at any time subsequent to the execution of this Contract by the parties hereto.

5. REAL ESTATE TAXES:

Real estate taxes to the County Treasurer shall remain In the Vendor's name throughout the term of this agreement. Payment of said taxes shall be the responsibility of the Vendee upon the execution of this agreement, and [____] shall [____] shall not be escrowed and added to the payment required by Vendee herein.

6. INSURANCE AND MAINTENANCE:

The Vendor shall insure the property with a non owner-occupant (landlord) policy against fire and extended coverage to the benefit of both parties as their Interests may appear herein. Said policy shall be for an amount no less than _____, payment of which shall be the responsibility of the Vendee, and which shall be escrowed and added to the payment due herein.

Vendees shall keep the building in a good state of repair at the Vendees expense. At such time as the Vendor inspects the premises and finds that repairs are necessary, Vendor shall request that these repairs be made within sixty (60) days at the Vendees expense.
The Vendees have inspected the premises constituting the subject matter of this Land Contract, and no representations have been made to the Vendee by the Vendor in regard to the condition of said premises: and it is agreed that the said premises are being sold to the Vendee as the same now exists and that the Vendor shall have no obligation to do or furnish anything toward the improvement of said premises.

Vendor shall furnish a clear termite report at Vendor's expense prior to executing this contract. If the property has live infestation of wood destroying insec1s, Vendor will pay costs of treatment and repair damages caused by same. If Vendor elects not to do so. Vendee may elect to waive Vendors responsibility and proceed. Vendee may elect not to proceed with this contract. Notice of each election shall be given in writing within five (5) days of. respectively. receipt of Vendor of the notice of infestation and receipt by Vendee of Vendors notice as to intention to remedy.

7.   POSSESSION

The Vendee shall be given possession of the above described premises at Contract execution and shall thereafter have and hold the same subject to default provisions hereinafter set forth.

8.   Delivery of DEED:

Upon full payment of this contract, Vendor shall issue a General Warranty deed to the Vendees free of all encumbrances except as otherwise set forth. In addition, Vendees reserves the right to convert this contract into a note and mortgage which shall bear the same terms as the contract for the remaining balance, and receive a warranty Deed to Vendees or assigns from Vendor, anytime the following conditions have been met by then Vendees,

1.   At least 20% of the purchase price has been paid to the Vendor.

2.   Vendee is willing to pay all the costs of title transfer and document preparations.

9.   DEFAULT BY VENDEES

If an installment payment to be made by the Vendee under the terms of this Land Contract is not paid by the Vendee when due or within thirty (30) days thereafter, the entire unpaid balance shall become due and collectable at the election of the Vendor and the Vendor shall be entitled to all the remedies provided for by the laws of this state and/or to do any other remedies and/or seek relief now or hereafter provided for by law to such Vendor; and in the event of the breach of this contract in any other respect by the Vendee, Vendor shall be entitled to all relief now or hereinafter provided for by the laws of this state.

Failure of Vendee to maintain current the status of all real estate taxes and insurance premiums as required herein shall permit Vendor the option to pay any such premiums, taxes, interest, or penalty (ies), and to add the amount paid to the principal amount owing under this contract, or to exercise any remedies available to the Vendor as per the preceding paragraph.

Waiver by the Vendor of a default or a number of defaults in the performance hereof by the Vendee shall not be construed as a waiver of any future default no matter how similar.

10. GENERAL PROVISIONS:

There are no known pending orders issued by any governmental authority with respect to this property other than those spelled out in this Land Contract prior to closing date for the execution of the contract.

11. SPECIAL PROVISIONS:

_____
_____
_____

12. ENTIRE AGREEMENT:

It is agreed that this instrument and any addendum mutually entered into and, by reference to this agreement, made a part hereof constitutes the entire agreement of the parties, and which shall be binding upon each of the parties, their administrators. executors, heirs, and assigns. It is further agreed that neither party is relying upon any representation not contained herein.

OPTION AGREEMENT FOR PURCHASE OF REAL PROPERTY

THIS OPTION AGREEMENT ("Agreement") made and entered into this _____ day of _____, 20_____, by and between _____, whose principal address is _____, hereinafter referred to as "Seller" and _____, whose principal address is _____, hereinafter referred to as "Purchaser":

W I T N E S S E T H:

WHEREAS, Seller is the fee simple owner of certain real property being, lying and situated in the County of _____, State of _____, such real property having the street address of _____ ("Premises") and such property being more particularly described as follows:

_____and,

WHEREAS, Purchaser desires to procure an option to purchase the Premises upon the terms and provisions as hereinafter set forth.

NOW, THEREFORE, for good and valuable consideration the receipt and sufficiency of which is hereby acknowledged by the parties hereto and for the mutual covenants contained herein, Seller and Purchaser hereby agree as follows:

1. DEFINITIONS

For the purposes of this Agreement, the following terms shall have the following meanings:

(a) "Execution Date" shall mean the day upon which the last party to this Agreement shall duly execute this Agreement

(b) "Option Fee" shall mean the total sum of a down payment of _____ percent (___%) of the total purchase price of the Premises plus all closing costs, payable as set forth below;

(c) "Option Term" shall mean that period of time commencing on the Execution Date and ending on or before _____, 20____

(d) "Option Exercise Date" shall mean that date, within the Option Term, upon which the Purchaser shall send its written notice to Seller exercising its Option to Purchase

(e) "Closing Date" shall mean the last day of the closing term or such other date during the closing term selected by Purchaser.

2. GRANT OF OPTION.

For and in consideration of the Option Fee payable to Seller as set forth herein, Seller does hereby   grant to Purchaser the exclusive right and Option ("Option") to purchase the premises upon the   terms and conditions as set forth herein.

3. PAYMENT OF OPTION FEE

Purchaser agrees to pay the Seller a down payment of _____ percent (_____%) of the total purchase price of the Premises plus all closing costs upon the Execution Date.

4. EXERCISE OF OPTION

Purchaser may exercise its exclusive right to purchase the Premises pursuant to the Option, at any time during the Option Term, by giving written notice thereof to Seller. As provided for above, the date of sending of said notice shall be the Option Exercise Date. In the event the Purchaser does not exercise its exclusive right to purchase the Premises granted by the Option during the Option Term, Seller shall be entitled to retain the Option Fee, and this agreement shall become absolutely null and void and neither party hereto shall have any other liability, obligation, or duty herein under or pursuant to this Agreement.

5. CONTRACT FOR PURCHASE & SALE OF REAL PROPERTY

In the event that the Purchaser exercises its exclusive Option as provided for in   the preceding paragraph, Seller agrees to sell and Purchaser agrees to buy the Premises and both parties agree to execute a contract for such purchase and sale of the Premises in accordance with the following terms and conditions:

(a) Purchase Price. The purchase price for the Premises shall be the sum of _____ ($_____); however, Purchaser shall receive a credit toward such purchase price in the amount of the Option Fee thus, Purchaser shall pay to Seller at closing the sum of _____ ($_____);

(b) Closing Date The closing date shall be on _____, 20_____ or at any other date during the Option Term as may be selected by Purchaser

(c) Closing Costs Purchaser's and Seller's costs of closing the Contract shall be borne by Purchase and shall be prepaid as a portion of the Option Fee;

(d) Default by Purchaser; Remedies of Seller. In the event Purchaser, after exercise of the Option, fails to proceed with the closing of the purchase of the Premises pursuant to the terms and provisions as contained herein and/or under the Contract, Seller shall be entitled to retain the Option Fee as liquidated damages and shall have no further recourse against Purchaser;

(e) Default by Seller; Remedies of Purchaser. In the event Seller fails to close the sale of the Premises pursuant to the terms and provisions of this Agreement and/or under the Contract, Purchaser shall be entitled to either sue for specific performance of the real estate purchase and sale contract or terminate such Contract and sue for money damages.

6. MISCELLANEOUS

(a) Execution by Both Parties This Agreement shall not become effective and binding until fully executed by both Purchaser and Seller.

(b) Notice All notices, demands, and/or consents provided for in this Agreement shall be in writing and shall be delivered to the parties hereto by hand or by United States Mail with postage pre-paid. Such notices shall be deemed to have been served on the date mailed, postage pre-paid. All such notices and communications shall be addressed to the Seller at _____ and to Purchaser at _____ or at such other address as either may specify to the other in writing.

(c) Fee Governing Law This Agreement shall be governed by and construed in accordance with the laws of the State of _____.

(d) Successors and Assigns This Agreement shall apply to, inure to the benefit of, and be binding upon and enforceable against the parties hereto and their respective heirs, successors, and or assigns, to the extent as if specified at length throughout this Agreement.

(e) Time is of the essence of this Agreement.

(f) Headings The headings inserted at the beginning of each paragraph and/or subparagraph are for convenience of reference only and shall not limit or otherwise affect or be used in the construction of any terms or provisions hereof.

(g) Cost of this Agreement Any cost and/or fees incurred by the Purchaser or Seller in executing this Agreement shall be borne by the respective party incurring such cost and/or fee.

(h) Entire Agreement This Agreement contains all of the terms, promises, covenants, conditions and representations made or entered into by or between Seller and Purchaser and supersedes all prior discussions and agreements whether written or oral between Seller and Purchaser with respect to the Option and all other matters contained herein and constitutes the sole and entire agreement between Seller and Purchaser with respect thereto. This Agreement may not be modified or amended unless such amendment is set forth in writing and executed by both Seller and Purchaser with the formalities hereof.

IN WITNESS WHEREOF, the parties hereto have caused this Agreement to be executed under proper authority:

As to Purchaser this _____ day of _____, 20_____

Witnesses: "Purchaser"

_____   _____

As to Seller this _____ day of _____, 20_____

Witnesses: "Seller"

_____   _____

Agreement to Lease with Option to Purchase

Parties:

Buyer _____ of _____

and

Seller_____ of _____

In consideration of the payments, covenants, agreements and conditions herein contained the above parties hereby agree to lease with an option the following property:

Subject: Property Address:_____

Legal Description: _____
_____

Personal Property _____
Personal property to be transferred at closing by bill of sale free of any encumbrances.

Existing Loans- At time of closing buyer may elect to take title subject to the existing loans to_____ In the amount of $_____ bearing interest rate of _____% payable _____ (P&I) Or the loan will be paid off by the seller.

Loan Number_____ Date last payment made_____
Other Liens, back taxes, etc._____
Term of lease and option _____months beginning _____
Monthly Payment $_____due on the _____day of each month beginning _____ 20____

Monthly credit toward purchase price when rent paid on time $_____

Purchase Price $_____, additional option consideration _____to apply towards purchase price.

1. TERMS: Seller agrees that upon the exercise of the option they will assist in financing by taking as part of the purchase price a note in the amount of

$\underline{\hspace{3cm}}$ with payments of $\underline{\hspace{3cm}}$ beginning
$\underline{\hspace{3cm}}$.

2. MAINTENANCE: The buyers shall pay for all repairs costing less than $ 100.00 each month. Repairs costing $100 or more will be paid by the owner. Should the owner fail to make repairs to maintain the house in its current condition, the buyer may have said repairs made and receive a credit equal to 200% of the cost of the repair toward the purchase price and a full credit toward the next payment due.

3. SELLER'S AGREEMENT NOT TO FURTHER ENCUMBER: Sellers agree not to refinance the property, nor to modify any existing loans, nor to transfer any interest in the property during the term of this agreement.

4. PAYMENTS ON EXISTING LOANS, TAXES AND INSURANCE: Seller shall be responsible for paying the taxes, loan payments and for keeping the property insured for its full replacement value during the term of this agreement. In the event seller fails to make payments when due of taxes, insurance, or loan payments, buyer may elect to make said pays due payments and receive 200% of their amount credited toward the purchase price and full credit toward the next payment due the seller.

5. PRORATIONS: Taxes, insurance, and loan interest shall be prorated as of the date of closing of the purchase.

6. BUYER & SELLER: agree to fully execute and place in escrow with $\underline{\hspace{4cm}}$ instruments needed to convey title. The seller shall deposit and executed warranty deed, and copies of existing mortgages, notes, title insurance policies, and surveys. Buyer shall deposit an executed quitclaim deed that will be delivered to the seller in the event of default by the buyer under this contract. All agree to sign an escrow agreement that will empower the escrow agent to close the transaction if all terms of the contract are met, and that will hold the agent harmless.

7. TRANSFER OF TITLE: In the event buyer chooses to exercise their option to purchase, they will notify the seller during the term of this agreement. Within 15 days of receipt of such notice, sellers agree to convey good and marketable title, free from all encumbrances except those that a buyer wishes to take title subject to. Sellers further agree to furnish an owner's title binder within 5 days after receiving notice, showing no exceptions other than as listed above, and furnish a policy of title insurance at closing.

8. DAMAGES: In the event seller fails to perform, buyer will be entitled to recover all monies paid on this agreement, and may pursue all other legal remedies available.

Seller will be responsible for all costs including a reasonable attorney's fee. In the event buyer fails to exercise the option, all option consideration, and rents paid will be forfeited as full-liquidated damages.

9. RECORDING: All parties agree that this agreement or a memorandum including any parts of their agreement acceptable to the buyer may be recorded.

10. SUCCESSORS AND ASSIGNS & SUBLETTING: The terms and conditions of this contract shall bind all successors, heirs, administrators, executors, assigns, and those subletting.

11. ACCESS AND ADVERTISING: Sellers agree that the buyer may advertise the property and shall immediately have access during reasonable hours to show the property to others.

12. TIME IS OF THE ESSENCE IN ALL MATTERS OF THE AGREEMENT

13. OTHER TERMS:

_____

_____

_____

_____

_____

The undersigned agree to buy and sell on the above terms, have-read, fully understand and verify the above information as being correct. All parties acknowledge that this is a legally binding contract and are advised to seek the counsel of an attorney.

Seller: _____ Date: _____

Seller: _____ Date: _____

Buyer _____ Date: _____

Buyer _____ Date: _____

State of _____ County of _____

www.ingramcontent.com/pod-product-compliance
Lightning Source LLC
Chambersburg PA
CBHW082357270326
41935CB00013B/1653